RED B(

Wide Range Readers
Readers

Phyllis Flowerdew

Oliver & Boyd

Illustrated by Virginia Smith

Acknowledgements

'The Firebird' is adapted from a story in *Folk Tales from North America* by Peter Lum, published by Frederick Muller Ltd. 'What Happened to the Forest?' is adapted from a story in *French Legends, Tales and Fairy Stories* retold by Barbara Leonie Picard, published by Oxford University Press (1955), and is reproduced by permission of the publisher.

OLIVER & BOYD
Pearson Education Limited
Edinburgh Gate
Harlow
Essex CM20 2JE
An Imprint of Longman Group UK Ltd

First published 1979
Eighteenth impression 1999

© Phyllis Flowerdew 1979
All rights reserved. No part of this publication may be
reproduced, stored in a retrieval system, or transmitted in
any form or by any means, electronic, mechanical,
photocopying, recording, or otherwise, without either the prior
written permission of the Publishers or a licence permitting
restricted copying issued by the Copyright Licensing Agency
Ltd, 90 Tottenham Court Road, London, W1P OLP.

ISBN 0 05 003189 9

Printed in Singapore (FOP)
WP/14

The publisher's policy is to use paper manufactured from
sustainable forests.

PREFACE

There are six Wide Range Readers Red Books. They can be used alone or with Wide Range Readers Blue and Green, with which they are parallel. The controlled vocabulary and graded sentence structure makes them suitable for children with the following reading ages:

7 to $7\frac{1}{2}$ years	–	Book 1
$7\frac{1}{2}$ to 8 years	–	Book 2
8 to $8\frac{1}{2}$ years	–	Book 3
$8\frac{1}{2}$ to 9 years	–	Book 4
9 to 10 years	–	Book 5
10 to 11+ years	–	Book 6

The success of Wide Range Blue and Green Books has been proved through the years, and the author hopes that the addition of the Red series will bring pleasure to teachers and children.

Phyllis Flowerdew

Contents

Verdi 5
A Cave Child's Toys 15
The Hotel Cat 16
Night in the Park 30
The King's Heart 32
The Man Who Wouldn't Move – Part 1 40
The Man Who Wouldn't Move – Part 2 51
A Page of Riddles 60
The Firebird 61
Out with the Tide 70
A Tree for the Roof 71
Poor Old Car 84
What Happened to the Forest? 85
Cartwheels 96
The Duck Village 99
The Three Golden Hairs – Part 1 112
The Three Golden Hairs – Part 2 121

Verdi

"I'll have to go to church early next Sunday," said the little Italian boy, Verdi, to his mother and father. "I'm going to help the priest."

"What are you going to do?" asked his mother.

"Oh, all the things that Marco used to do," he replied. "He's left now. I shall carry the candles, and stand by the altar and hand things to the priest during the services. I shall wear a special robe too."

"That will be nice," said his mother. Her son was only seven years old, and she felt proud that he had been chosen. Verdi's father felt proud too, but that did not make him like the priest any better. He was not good and patient as a priest should be. He lost his temper easily, and there were many people in the village who did not like him.

"Listen carefully to what he tells you," warned Verdi's father, "so that you don't make any mistakes."

The little boy, Verdi, liked the village church with its richly-coloured walls and its high curved ceiling. There were pictures and painted carvings of saints and angels and fat little cherubs with tiny wings. There were pictures of blue sky, fluffy white clouds and shafts of dazzling light.

He soon learned what he had to do for the different services. Sometimes he had to light the lamps. Sometimes he had to carry the long white candles and put them in their places. Sometimes he had to pass the holy water or the wine to the priest at the altar.

For several weeks all went well. Then there came a Sunday when things were rather different. Perhaps Verdi was more dreamy than usual on that day. Perhaps the priest was more grumpy than usual.

Verdi stood by the altar helping with the service. He knew exactly what he had to do, but instead of watching the priest, he was listening to the organ.

He always liked the organ. Its loud, deep, swelling notes rose to the very roof. They echoed and trembled in every corner. They filled the whole church with a great surge of sound.

"How beautiful it is," thought Verdi. He should, at that moment, have passed a dish of holy water to the priest. The priest waited for it. What was this silly little boy, Verdi, doing? He was just staring at the ceiling.

"Water," whispered the priest, but Verdi did not move. He just went on staring at the ceiling. He felt as if he had wings like the fat little cherubs. He felt as if he were flying with the painted angels, up to the painted sky.

"Water," hissed the priest, but still Verdi did not move. He just went on staring at the ceiling. He felt as if he were lying back on the painted clouds, listening to the organ music.

"Wake up, boy," muttered the priest

angrily and he gave the little boy a rough push. Perhaps he pushed harder than he meant to do. Perhaps Verdi was not standing very firmly on his feet. He lost his balance. He stumbled and fell. He went tumbling down the altar steps. He landed in a painful, crumpled heap at the bottom.

A gasp went through the church. Everyone looked in horror. Fancy the *priest* pushing the poor little boy, Verdi, down the steps! Fancy pushing him over in *church!*

After the service, everyone was talking about it. The news reached Verdi's mother and father even before he reached home himself.

"I'll have something to say to that priest when I see him," said his father angrily.

"Are you hurt?" asked his mother anxiously. Yes, he was hurt. He had several bruises, and his leg was bleeding. "Oh, it's nothing," he replied. It was not important. He was thinking of something else. He wanted to ask his mother and father something. It was something he wanted more than anything he had ever wanted before.

"Please, please may I learn to play the organ?" he asked.

Verdi's father kept a small inn and a little village shop, but he did not make much money out of them. All the same, if Verdi wanted to learn the organ, he would manage to pay for lessons somehow. So, in a very short time, the church organist was giving Verdi lessons on the church organ.

"Your son is very good," the organist told Verdi's father after a few weeks. "He learns so quickly. In fact it almost seems as if he knows everything before I explain it to him."

Then a wonderful thing happened. Verdi's father bought him an old spinet so that he could play on it at home. A spinet was something like a very small piano and was played in rather the same way. Nothing could have made the little boy happier.

He played the church music that the organist taught him. He played the tunes he sometimes heard people singing in his father's inn. And he played his own music, music that just came into his head and went down to his fingers. Music became the most important thing in his life.

One day when Verdi was ten years old, the organist said to him,

"I shall not be able to play for the service on Sunday morning, so I want you to take my place."

"But I've never played when the church has been full of people," replied Verdi.

"I know, but you'll do it, won't you? You'll do it well."

"All right. I'll do it."

So, the next Sunday, Verdi sat at the church organ and looked round at the richly-coloured walls and the high curved ceiling. He looked at the painted carvings of saints and angels and fat little cherubs with tiny wings. He looked at the pictures of blue sky and the fluffy white clouds and the shafts of dazzling light.

Then it was time to begin. He pressed the pedals with his feet. He spread his small hands over the black and white keys. He played. He sent the deep, swelling notes rising to the very roof. They echoed and trembled in every corner. They filled the whole church with a great surge of sound.

At first some of the people did not know that the organist was missing. Then one by one they looked up, and noticed, and began to whisper to each other,

"Look who is playing the organ. It's the little boy, Verdi."

. . . .

Verdi grew up to be a good, kind man, loved and honoured in Italy and in other countries too. He spent his life making music, as he had done since childhood. He wrote beautiful, solemn music to be played and sung in church.

He also wrote operas to be acted on the stage. Operas are plays in which the actors sing their parts instead of saying them. He became the greatest writer of opera music in Italy, and his music is still played again and again throughout the world.

A Cave Child's Toys

Berries, beans
    And whitened bones,
 Sticks and shells
    And coloured stones,
Balls of mud
    And dolls of clay,
These would be there
    For your play.

Seeds to rattle
    In your hand,
Twigs to draw with
    On the sand,
Leaves to sail
    Where rivers flow,
These your games
    Of long ago.

The Hotel Cat

The white hotel stood on the hillside with its windows staring out like eyes over the valley below. In the spring and summer it was full of people. They came to see the country from their cars, or to spend their holidays tramping over the hills. There were maids and cooks and cleaners to look after them all.

But in the autumn, when the last visitors had gone, the hotel closed down, and the maids and cooks and cleaners went away.

Then the building stood empty and lonely all through the winter.

Judy was always a little afraid of it in the autumn and winter. It looked so sad, and sometimes the wind howled round it from end to end. It rattled at the closed windows and moaned in the chimneys.

Of course there was no need for her to go past it at all, but it was the only building anywhere near her own cottage. Besides it was on the way to the woods.

"I'm going for a walk," she said one day to her mother. It was a Sunday in autumn and she had a week's holiday from school. She walked slowly up the hill to the hotel. It had closed down only the day before. The windows were locked. The doors were locked. The people had gone. The hotel was empty.

Judy shivered. The air was full of sounds. There were dry leaves rustling. There were branches creaking in the forest, and there was another sound. It was a crying, a mewing; and there, from the shelter of the porch at this end of the hotel, came a cat. It was a large, ginger cat. It walked up to Judy and rubbed itself against her legs. It seemed very glad to see her.

"Someone in the hotel must have left

it behind," Judy thought. She stroked the cat gently and said,

"Come home with me," but the cat would not follow her. Then, when at last Judy went home without it, the cat stood and watched her, mewing sadly as if trying to call her back.

. . . . . .

The next day Judy walked to the white hotel again. This time her mother had given her a small plastic dish and a little plastic bottle full of milk.

"I hope I see the cat again," she thought. It was a windy day and the air was full of flying leaves; and the forest shone with all the colours of autumn. Judy stood still and looked towards the porch for the cat, but she could not see it. She called, and her voice echoed round the empty hotel, but the cat did not come.

Then there was a flurry of dry,

dancing leaves in the porch, and there it was! It stood up and stretched itself.

"Hello," said Judy. "I've brought some milk for you." The cat came forward to meet her. It rubbed itself against her legs, and Judy stroked it. She walked into the porch and put the plastic dish down beside a pile of autumn leaves. She poured the milk into it. The cat put out its little pink tongue and lapped at it.

"You poor thing," said Judy. "You are very thirsty, aren't you?" She watched its tongue going in and out. She watched the milk sinking lower and lower in the dish. Then she noticed a movement in the pile of leaves – a tiny, struggling, unsteady movement.

"Oh!" she whispered. "A kitten!" It was small and young, with eyes tightly closed, and a worried little creased-up face. And beside it there was another, and another, and another – four tiny kittens in a nest of dry leaves!

They all had their eyes tightly closed. They all had worried little creased-up faces. No wonder the cat had not followed Judy home yesterday! It had four little kittens to look after, here in the porch at the hotel.

After a while, just as Judy was thinking of going back home, a van drew up at the back of the hotel. Two men jumped out and unlocked the door. They carried ladders and buckets and tins of paint inside.

Judy wondered whether to go up to them and say, "Don't touch the kittens, will you," but she was shy, and the men had not seen her, so she went away without saying anything at all.

That evening, sitting by the fire at home, Judy said to her mother and father,

"Shall we bring the cat and kittens here tomorrow, so that we can look after them?"

"I don't quite know what is the best thing to do," said Mother.

"What do you think, Daddy?" asked Judy, but Father did not answer. He was listening to the wind howling in the trees.

"Sounds like a storm coming up," he said.

The cottage was warm and cosy, but the night outside was dark and wild. Even as Father spoke, the wind grew louder. The trees moaned and creaked, and the air was filled with strange, unhappy sounds.

"I've never heard such a strong wind," said Mother, and she pulled aside the curtains and looked out into the darkness.

"The hotel!" she screamed. "It's on

fire!" The wind was loud, but the roar of the fire was louder still. Flames spread from end to end of the hotel, blazing, leaping, crackling.

"Put on your coats and stay here," said Father. "If the wind changes, the cottage might be in danger. I'll go and see what I can do." He ran out of doors, pulling on his coat as he went. At the same time, Mother and Judy heard the wail of the fire engines as they came up from the village below.

"The kittens! The kittens!" cried Judy.

"Don't worry about them," said Mother. "They may be safe. You see, the flames are blowing away from the porch end, not towards it." She tried to comfort Judy, but she knew the heat of the fire must be very fierce, and the kittens would be very lucky if they were still alive.

Mother and Judy looked through the windows for a long time. They watched the firemen and saw the great spurts of

water from their hoses. They watched
until the hotel was a black and burned
framework against the glow of the dying
fire.

At last Judy fell asleep in an
armchair and Mother wrapped her in a
blanket, but Mother went on looking out of
the window. She watched the flames die
down, and heard the crash of falling
beams and tumbling walls. She smelled
the strong smell of black smoke, and she

felt very sad to think, that after all these years, the hotel had gone.

Then Father came in with two men from the village. Mother made them some hot cocoa, and Judy woke up and listened to them talking.

"I wonder how it started," said Mother.

"I suppose it was the painters," replied one of the men. "Perhaps they dropped a cigarette end, or a lighted match. Thank God no one was living there."

"And what about the cat and kittens?" asked Mother. Father shook his head. He had looked all around for them but he had not seen a sign of them. He had no hope at all.

. . . . . .

It was not until the end of the week that Judy went to see the hotel, for there was still a danger of falling bricks and beams, and the air was thick with drifting smoke. She went on Saturday with Mother and Father. They stood and looked at the burnt-out shell of the building. Walls had tumbled. Window frames had fallen out. Doors had gone. It was a sad, black scene.

"The porch is still standing," said Judy at once.

"It's no good looking in it," said Father. "I've looked lots of times."

Judy stared at the porch standing up by itself in a heap of tumbled ruins. Poor little cat! Poor little kittens!

"Look!" whispered Mother at that moment. Judy looked. Out of the woods came a cat, a large, ginger cat. It walked up to Judy and rubbed itself against her legs as if very glad to see her.

"My cat!" murmured Judy, and she could hardly believe her eyes. "My cat! It's safe!" But what about the kittens? They had been too young to run to safety.

The cat walked away a few steps and then walked back to Judy. Then it walked away again.

"Watch where it goes," said Mother. So Judy followed the cat. It walked into the wood. So Judy walked into the wood, and behind her went Mother and Father, stepping as quietly as they could on dry leaves and crackling twigs.

"Look!" whispered Judy. "It has made itself a nest." It was a little mossy hollow full of dry leaves. The leaves were red and yellow and brown and gold – all the colours of autumn; and among the leaves there were movements, tiny, struggling, unsteady movements.

The kittens! There they were, with
eyes still tightly closed, and worried
little creased-up faces. They were all
safe and sound in a nest of dry leaves!

"The kittens!" cried Judy in
delight. "How did they get here?"

"The cat must have carried them, one
by one, in its mouth," explained
Father. "Perhaps it carried them
beyond the reach of the flames first,
and then carried them again, one by one,
into the woods."

"Brave, clever cat!" said Mother.
"It may even have sensed danger and
moved the kittens before the fire even began."

"They're rather like autumn leaves
themselves," said Judy – "that yellowy, ginger,
browny colour. They've grown a bit too."

. . . . .

The next day the owner of the hotel
came by car and called at the cottage
and spoke to Mother. He asked a few
questions about the fire, then he said,

"Have you seen anything of a cat? My housekeeper is very unhappy about it. It was expecting kittens, and she couldn't find it when she left the hotel. She had intended coming back today to have another look for it."

"Oh, it's safe," said Mother, "and so are the kittens." She told the story of the brave cat, and she added,

"If your housekeeper wants a home for any of the kittens, I know a girl who would love to have one." And so Judy, of course, ended up with one of the yellowy, ginger, browny kittens of the hotel cat.

Night in the Park

One summer evening
When it was dark,
A little boy squeezed
Through the gates of the park.

He played in the sand pit,
Silent and cool.
He dabbled his toes
In the paddling pool.

He slid down the slide,
Shining under the stars.
He hung upside down
On the parallel bars.

He swung on a swing,
Swinging low, swinging high,
And stared at the moon
Sailing gold in the sky.

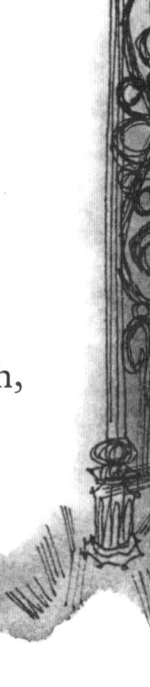

Then he squeezed out again
Through the gates of the park,
And the swing went on swinging
Alone in the dark.

The   went   swinging
    swing   on

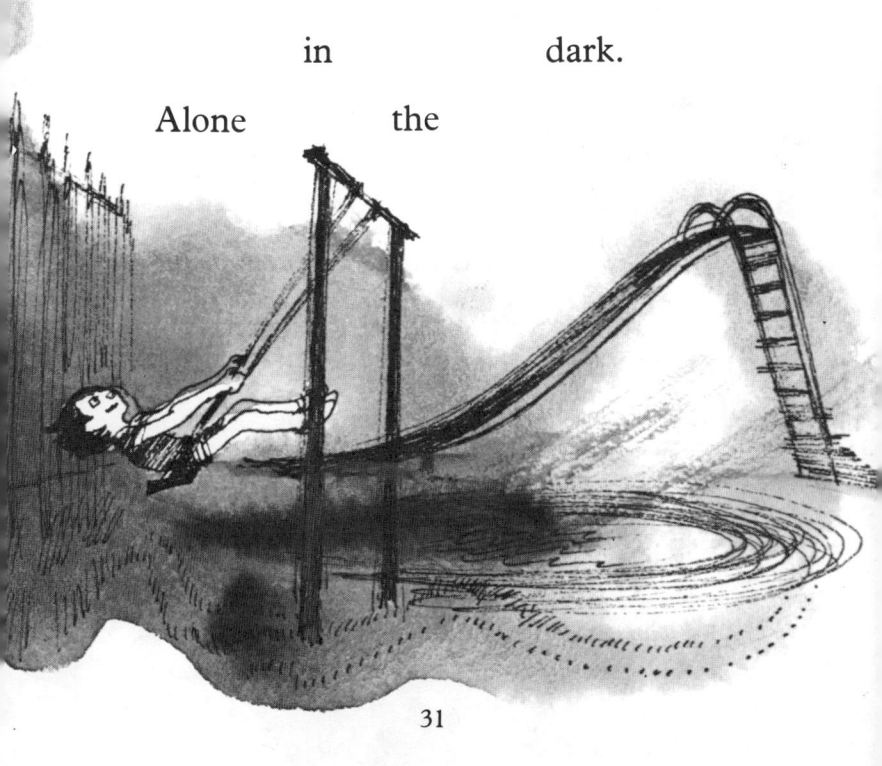

           in   dark.
   Alone   the

The King's Heart

Once upon a time there was a king who wanted to build a cathedral. He wanted it to be the biggest and most beautiful in the land. So the plans were drawn, and his workmen began to dig. Soon the foundations were dug and the first stones were laid, one upon the other. Even this took many months.

Then as the walls began to rise, the king found that his money was nearly all gone. There would never be enough to build a cathedral. What could he do? The only way to get more money would be to tax the people, and he did not want to do that. He felt very unhappy about it, and he walked slowly along in the mountains trying to think what to do.

Suddenly a little man appeared in front of him. There was something rather strange about him, and he looked up at the king and said,

"Why do you look so sad?"

"I have started to build a great cathedral," replied the king, "and I haven't the money to finish it."

"Don't worry about that," said the little man. "I will build it for you. I will build the biggest and most beautiful cathedral in the land, and I will not ask you for any money."

The king felt very surprised at this.

"What will you want for payment?" he asked.

"If you can guess my name by the time I have finished your church, I shall not want any payment at all," said the little man. "But if you cannot guess my name, you must give me your heart."

"My heart!" exclaimed the king. Surely the little man would not really take his heart! It seemed such an impossible thing that the king did not give it much thought. The cathedral would take years and years to build. He might even be dead by then. So he said,

"All right. I promise." The little man nodded, and then disappeared.

"He must be a gnome," thought the king, for in those days there were strange little people living hidden in the mountains.

Next day the king told his own workmen to stop building, and he gave them other jobs to do. He walked over to the cathedral, but there was no one near it. He looked at the foundations. He looked at the low walls. There was no work being done. There was no one in sight.

That night when it was dark, he went again. This time there was the sound of little voices and the tapping of tiny tools. The king looked at the foundations. He looked at the low walls. Everywhere there were little gnomes, carrying stones, mixing mortar, slapping and tapping with tiny tools. Everywhere there were strange little men, working, working, building, building.

No work was ever done on the cathedral by day; but every night the gnome-builders came out and went on building. The walls rose high, higher, higher. Great windows were put in. Doors were made. The roof beams were set in place. Night by night the cathedral grew as if by magic.

Now the king began to feel worried about the promise he had made to the little man in the mountains.

"The whole building will be finished in a few days," he thought, so he said to the little man,

"I should like some rich carving on the stone work. I should like some statues set in place round the walls. I should like a very tall spire."

"All right," said the little man. "You shall have them."

The king tried to think of more ways to slow down the building, but whenever he asked for something extra, it would be finished the next night.

Now there was rich carving on the stone work. Now there were statues set in place round the walls. Now there was a very tall spire. It rose and rose. It came to a thin point at the top. The cathedral was almost finished.

The king walked into the mountains and wondered what to do. What else could he ask for, to slow down the building? It was evening and the gnomes would soon be back at work, perhaps for the last time. How could he guess the little man's name? How could he possibly give up his heart?

Suddenly he heard the sound of crying. It was coming from a cave near by. There must be a baby there. Yet it did not sound quite like the cry of a human baby. It must be a baby gnome.

The king stood still and listened. Then he heard another voice. It was the voice of the gnome baby's mother. She was singing softly, and trying to hush and comfort the baby.

"Don't cry my little one," she said. "Tomorrow your Daddy will bring a king's heart for you to play with. Old Foul Weather, your father, will bring a king's heart for you."

Old Foul Weather! Now the king knew the little man's name! He walked quietly away from the cave and he hurried to the cathedral. By the time he reached it, darkness was falling. There was only one gnome on the building, and that was the little man himself. He was perched on the tip of the spire, fixing a golden weathercock in place. It was the very last thing he had to do.

"Hello!" called the king loudly, looking

up at the spire. "Mind you put the weathercock on straight, Old Foul Weather!"

At the sound of his name, the little man fell crashing to the ground, and he must have been made of glass, for he broke into a thousand pieces.

As for the golden weathercock on the great cathedral, that has been crooked ever since.

Adapted

The Man Who Wouldn't Move – Part 1

Once upon a time there was an old man who was always known as Grandfather Green. He lived in a tumbledown cottage with his wife, Grandmother Green, and his three little grandchildren, Biggy, Middly and Baby. At the side of the cottage was a tumbledown stable, and in the stable Grandfather Green kept his horse, Blackberry.

Not far away, on the edge of the town, Grandfather Green had a plot of land where he grew cabbages and carrots. He used to ride out to it on Blackberry the horse. Then he would load Blackberry up with cabbages and carrots which he would take to the market to sell.

Now when Grandfather Green had been young, the tumbledown cottage had been in a green and grassy place in a row of other cottages. It had been in a small town with only a few shops, and hardly any traffic passing through.

But slowly over the years the other cottages in the row had tumbled down. New town houses had been built. There were streets and streets of them, grey and ugly and all huddled together as if they were trying to keep warm.

The town grew too. It grew from a small place to a large and busy city with shops and offices and factories. Cars and lorries began to rattle through from morning till night.

But in the middle of all this,

Grandfather Green's tumbledown cottage still stood. Its thatched roof was wearing into holes. Its bricks were cracking. Its wooden beams were crumbling. It still stood with the tumbledown stable beside it and a tiny garden round it. It looked like part of an old world in the middle of a new world.

Now people who build cities never leave them alone for very long. They are always making new plans and changing old plans. They are always building new shops and changing old shops. Then, as more and more people flock into the city to work, they have to build more and more houses for them.

So, one day Biggy, Middly and Baby came running into the tumbledown cottage with some news. They had been playing in the street with some of the children who lived in the grey and ugly houses that all huddled together as if they were trying to keep warm.

"Grandfather," said Biggy, "they're going to take all the houses down round here, and build big, new blocks of flats, and a great estate of council houses, stretching from here to the market."

"Yes," added Middly, "and they're going to take our cottage down too."

"Yes," murmured Baby, who seldom said anything that was not just an echo of what Biggy and Middly had said before.

"Oh dear!" sighed Grandmother. "I wonder if it's true."

"Rubbish!" snapped Grandfather Green. "It's just rubbish."

But it was not rubbish, for soon everyone was talking about it. Soon some ground was cleared near the market, and soon building was started. Council houses seemed to be up in no time. They were neat little modern houses with neat little gardens waiting to be dug. There were rows and rows of houses waiting for people to move in and bring them to life.

Soon, letters were put through the doors of the grey and ugly houses that all huddled together as if they were trying to keep warm. The letters said,

> You must move out of your house within the next few weeks. A van will move your furniture free of charge. The address of your new council house will be . . . . .

Most people were very pleased. They moved as quickly as possible out of the ugly, grey houses and into the new council houses with their new shining bathrooms, and beautiful modern kitchens.

Workmen came and knocked down the ugly, grey houses that all huddled together as if they were trying to keep warm. They knocked them all down, and cleared the ground. Then they started putting up blocks of flats. They put up great blocks of flats with fourteen, sixteen, eighteen, twenty floors.

But in the middle of all this, Grandfather Green's tumbledown cottage still stood. Its thatched roof was wearing into holes. Its bricks were cracking. Its wooden beams were crumbling. It still stood with the tumbledown stable beside it and a tiny garden round it. It looked like part of an old world in the middle of a new world.

Then one day, Biggy, Middly and Baby came running in with news again.

"Grandfather," said Biggy, "they're going to start taking our cottage down in two weeks' time."

"Yes," said Middly, "and we shall move into a new council house with a new shining bathroom and a beautiful modern kitchen."

"Yes," murmured Baby, who seldom said anything that was not just an echo of what Biggy and Middly had said before.

"Oh dear," sighed Grandmother. "I wonder if there will be a stable there for Blackberry the horse."

"If there's not," snapped Grandfather Green, "we shall not move. We shall simply refuse to move."

But of course there wasn't a stable! None of the council houses had stables. The council house that was now ready for Grandfather Green and Grandmother Green and Biggy, Middly and Baby was called

Number Seven, Chestnut Road.

It was a neat little modern house with a neat little garden, waiting to be dug. The house was just waiting for the family to move in and bring it to life.

It had a fine large living-room and three fine bedrooms. It had a new shining bathroom and a beautiful modern kitchen, but it had no stable for Blackberry the horse.

"So we shall not move into it," said Grandfather Green. "We shall simply refuse to move."

A man called at the tumbledown cottage to ask Grandfather Green which day he would like the van to call for the furniture.

"No day, thank you," snapped Grandfather Green. "We shall not need it on any day. We refuse to move unless you build us a stable for our horse, Blackberry."

Soon another man called at the tumbledown cottage.

"I'm afraid you'll have to move out before April the third," he said to Grandfather Green. "On April the third, workmen will be coming here to take the cottage down."

"They can come on April the third," snapped Grandfather Green, "but they will not get us out. We refuse to move unless you build us a stable for our horse, Blackberry."

Early, early in the morning of April the third, Grandfather Green crept out of doors, led Blackberry the horse from the stable and took him inside the tumbledown cottage. Then he locked and bolted and barred the doors. He moved a cupboard up against the back door, and a chest of drawers up against the front door.

"Now let them try and move us out," he said. Grandmother was worried, and Biggy, Middly and Baby were frightened. They had their breakfast and waited.

Sure enough, there came a knock at the door. Rat-tat-tat! No one answered. No one moved. Not Grandfather Green, nor Grandmother Green. Not Biggy, Middly and Baby, not even Blackberry the horse.

The knock came again, louder. Rat-tat-tat! Still no one answered. Still no one moved. Then suddenly Grandfather Green shouted out in a voice that tore the silence apart like a thunder clap.

"Who are you? What do you want?"

"I'm sorry to trouble you sir," came a voice through the letter-box. "We have orders to start taking this cottage down today. Are you ready to come out now?"

"No, we are not!" shouted Grandfather Green. "We refuse to come out unless you build us a stable for our horse, Blackberry."

The workmen outside the door did not know what to do. They had orders to start taking the cottage down, but how could they take it down when there were people inside it? They stood about in the garden half the morning. They spoke to each other in low voices. Then they went away.

The Man Who Wouldn't Move – Part 2

Days and weeks passed and the great blocks of flats went slowly up and up, fourteen, sixteen, eighteen, twenty floors. All the old houses had gone. Everything became new and different, like a new city being made within an old city.

In the middle of all this, Grandfather Green's tumbledown cottage still stood. Its thatched roof was wearing into holes. Its bricks were cracking. Its wooden beams were crumbling. It still stood with the tumbledown stable beside it and the tiny garden round it, like part of an old world in the middle of a new world.

Now although Grandfather Green and the family were living in the cottage, the people who planned the city did not leave them alone. Oh no.

Every few days someone came banging

on the door asking the family to move.
Every few days workmen came shouting
through the letter-box, saying that they
had orders to take the cottage down.
Every few days Grandfather shouted back,

"We refuse to move unless you build us
a stable for our horse, Blackberry."

Grandfather was as brave as a lion,
and was quite sure no one would force
them out, but Grandmother was worried and
unhappy, and Biggy, Middly and Baby were
very, very frightened. They were so
frightened that they lay awake in their
beds at night and shivered.

The city newspaper told the story. It
showed a picture of the tumbledown
cottage. It told how Grandfather Green
would not leave it unless a stable were
built for his horse, Blackberry. Some of
the people who read the story thought he
must be a foolish old man, but others
smiled and thought, "Good old
Grandfather Green."

Then one day Biggy, Middly and Baby went for a walk. They walked up to the new council estate. They peeped through the windows of Number Seven, Chestnut Road. The house was still empty. It was still waiting for Grandfather Green and Grandmother Green and Biggy, Middly and Baby to move in and bring it to life.

"I wish we could move here," said Biggy.

"It's so nice," sighed Middly.

"Nice," murmured Baby, who seldom said anything that was not just an echo of what Biggy and Middly had said before.

They walked slowly away and wandered up and down the new roads, staring at the new houses. Most of them had curtains at the windows now, and some of the gardens had already been dug.

Suddenly they came to a high wooden fence, and a little later they came to a hole in it, just big enough for them to climb through. First they all put their heads through the hole and saw a small wood. Then they all climbed inside and went wandering through the trees.

They did not know it, but there was a big house there. In a way, it was like their own tumbledown cottage, because it also was like part of an old world in the middle of a new world. The house had stood there for hundreds of years all by itself, but now there were lots of streets and small modern houses round it.

Biggy, Middly and Baby had not seen the house yet but they came upon a barn with the door wide open. They peeped inside. There was a pile of straw at one end. Just then they heard someone coming. They heard footsteps.

"Hide in the straw," said Biggy, feeling suddenly afraid. Like three flashes of lightning, Biggy, Middly and Baby scrambled into the straw, and kept quite still.

The footsteps belonged to Mrs Page, the lady who lived in the big house. She had seen Biggy, Middly and Baby disappear into the barn and she felt very cross about it.

Her house and garden were like an island now in the middle of the council estate. Children were always peeping through the cracks in the fence. They had even made a big hole in it. She would have to get it mended or she would never have any peace.

Mrs Page went into the barn. She could not see the children anywhere. Then she saw an arm sticking out from the pile of straw. That was Biggy. Then she saw a leg sticking out from the pile of straw. That was Middly. Then she saw a little round face sticking out from the pile of straw. That was Baby.

"I can see you," said Mrs Page sternly. "Come out of the straw, all of you."

Out came Biggy. Out came Middly. Out came Baby.

"Naughty children, coming into my garden," went on Mrs Page. "I suppose you live in the new council houses."

"No," answered Biggy shyly. "There is a council house waiting for us in Chestnut Road but we have not moved into it."

"Because," explained Middly, "Grandfather refuses to move unless they build a stable for our horse, Blackberry."

"Blackberry," whispered Baby, who seldom said anything that was not just an echo of what Biggy and Middly had said before.

"Your horse, Blackberry!" exclaimed Mrs Page. "I read about it in the paper. Is your Grandfather known as Grandfather Green?"

"Yes," said Biggy, Middly and Baby.

"Mm," went on Mrs Page, "I read about him in the paper. I said to myself 'Good old Grandfather Green.' But they are still trying to get him to move, aren't they? He'll have to move out in the end." Then she paused, and looked round and said,

"Chestnut Road is only just round the corner from here. You would have found that out if you had gone to my front gate instead of climbing through the hole in

the fence. Do you think Grandfather
Green would like to keep your horse
Blackberry in this barn of mine?"

Biggy, Middly and Baby did not answer.
They were all too surprised to speak, and
the news seemed too good to be true.

"Well," said Mrs Page kindly, "do
you think your horse Blackberry would like
to sleep here at nights when you move into
your new house?"

"Oh, yes *please*," answered Biggy.

"*Thank* you," replied Middly.

"Please. Thank you," added Baby, who
seldom said anything that was not just an
echo of what Biggy and Middly had said before.

So it was all happily settled.
Grandfather Green and Grandmother Green
and Biggy, Middly and Baby moved into the
new council house at Number Seven,
Chestnut Road; and the horse Blackberry
spent the nights very comfortably indeed
in Mrs Page's barn, at the big house in
the middle of the council estate.

A Page of Riddles

Q. How does a ghost open a door?
A. With a skeleton key.

Q. Why is a batsman a coward?
A. Because he's afraid of a duck.

Q. What is the difference between someone who is greedy and someone who is hungry?
A. One eats too long and the other longs to eat.

Q. When is a shaggy dog most likely to enter a house?
A. When the door is open.

Q. Take away all my letters and I stay the same. What am I?
A. A postman.

The Firebird

There are many stories of how fire came to the world. This one was told by the Indians who lived in their wigwams and their houses of cedar wood on the west coast of Canada.

One day the people of the Indian tribe saw a strange bird flying above them. It was black and orange and it seemed as if little lights danced and played among the feathers of its long, shining tail. It flew very low as if it had a message to give to the people.

In those days, the Indians could speak the language of the animals and the birds, so one man called out,

"What bird are you, and why do you come here?"

"I am the firebird," came the answer. "I will give fire to the person who can catch it, and who will know how to use it wisely."

No one knew what the bird meant, for no one had heard of fire before.

"What is it?" they asked.

"It is like the light that dances and plays among the feathers of my tail. It will warm your homes. It will cook your food."

The Indians stretched out their hands and tried to catch the bird, but it flew always just beyond their reach. Then it said,

"Come here tomorrow, all of you, men, women and children. Bring a little bundle of pine wood, all of you, men,

women and children. Then follow me as I
fly. The one who can touch my tail with
his bundle of pine wood shall have the
fire."

"That should not be too hard," said
some of the men.

"But there is one other thing," added
the bird. "I cannot give the fire to
anyone who steals, or tells lies or who
has never done a kindness to his people."

Next morning the people stood together
outside their homes. There were men,
women and children, and each of them held
a little bundle of pine wood. The sky
was grey and the air was cold, and at
first there was no sign of the bird.

Then suddenly there was a flicker and
a flash and it appeared. It was black and
orange, and it seemed as if little lights
danced and played among the feathers of
its long, shining tail. It seemed, too,
as if it brought warmth with it.

"Now," said the bird, "I will fly

low, and you may follow." At once the Indians began to run along the valley where the bird led them. They leaped over stones. They slid in the mud. They tripped and stumbled on the rough ground. The bird flew very slowly. Yet it flew always just beyond their reach.

Some of the children grew tired very quickly. Some of them dropped their little bundles of pine wood and turned back home. Some of the old people could not keep up with the others. They, too, gave up the race.

More and more people gave up, until at last only a few men were left. They were the fastest runners in the tribe. Yet they could not catch the bird, for although it seemed to fly so slowly, it was always just beyond their reach.

At last one man caught up with the bird. He stretched out to touch its long, shining tail with his bundle of pine wood. He almost did it, but at that moment the firebird suddenly darted ahead again.

"Please, Firebird," said the man. "Give me the fire. I have run a long way. I almost caught you. I do not steal or tell lies, or do wrong to any of my people."

"That is true," replied the firebird. "You do not steal or tell lies, or do wrong. But you are selfish, and you never do a kindness to your people. I cannot give the fire to you."

So the first man turned back to the village and another fast runner came up close to the bird. He stretched out his hand to touch its long, shining tail with his bundle of pine wood. He almost did it, but at that moment the firebird suddenly darted ahead again.

"Please, Firebird," said the man. "Give me the fire. I have run a long way. I almost caught you. I have been kind to many people all my life."

"That is true," replied the firebird. "You have been kind to many people all your life, but in your wigwam is a piece of meat you took secretly from another man. I cannot give the fire to you."

So the second man turned back to the village and other men caught up in turn. But still the firebird did not give away the fire, for it knew that each person had, at some time, done something wrong. He had stolen something, or told a lie, or been unkind to one of his people. There seemed to be no one who could have the fire.

Sadly the bird flew over the village

again but it saw no one who could take the fire. It turned to fly away into the open country, but just then a woman called out from the doorway of a house of cedar wood. It was a lonely house, standing apart from the others.

"Firebird," called the woman. "Please give me the fire. I will use it wisely and I will share it with my people."

"You did not follow me," said the firebird. "You did not even gather a little bundle of pine wood. Why should I give the fire to you? What good have you done to others?"

"I have done nothing," replied the woman. "I have been too busy all these years. I have been looking after my children. I have been caring for my old mother, and nursing my sick father. I have never had time to help other people."

The firebird flew near so that the woman could almost touch it.

"Gather a little bundle of pine wood," said the bird. "Just a few twigs will do." So the woman picked up a few twigs of pine wood and put them in a little pile outside her door.

The firebird flew low and touched the twigs with its bright shining tail. Little lights played and danced among its feathers. Then suddenly little lights played and danced among the pine twigs. They grew into tiny flames, leaping bright and warm from twig to twig.

"Bring more pine wood," said the bird. The woman brought more wood and added it to the pile; and the flames spread and blazed and shone. There was fire at last, fire to warm the Indians' homes and to cook their food, and to pass and spread from one to another through the village.

And so it was that fire came to the world.

Adapted

Out With the Tide

Waves of the sea
 Flow in and out
Washing the shells
 Scattered about,
Splashing the rocks
 Where the jelly fish hide,
Telling the shrimps
 To come with the tide,
Calling the crabs
 That wait on the shore,
Taking them all
 To the ocean once more.

A Tree for the Roof

Karina was a Swiss girl. Her father was a builder, and he was working on a new house outside the town.

"It's in a beautful place," he said one day to Karina and her mother. "There are fields and wild flowers and forests all round, and in the distance there are great mountains capped with snow."

"Couldn't you take me there one day?" asked Karina, who was on holiday from school.

"Yes, I could," agreed Father slowly, "but you'd have to be there the whole day if you came. You could bring a book to read, and some drawing to do. The fresh air would do you good, I'm sure."

"When may I come?" asked Karina.

"Oh, some time soon," replied Father. Then he added quickly, "I tell you what. You can come on the day we put up the roof-tree. That will be one day next week. I'll ask Mr Stefan if it will be all right to take you."

"Oh yes," said Karina. "I should like that. The day the tree goes on the roof!"

Now in Switzerland and Germany and Poland there is an old, old custom. Whenever builders put the top beams of wood on the roof of a new house, they fix a tree or a bush on it. Sometimes they hang trails of coloured paper on the branches, so that it looks like a Christmas tree. It is supposed to bring blessings and good luck to the people who will live in the house.

When the roof-tree is up, the owner of the house comes to see it. He brings drinks for the builders, and they all feel happy and excited as if it is a party.

Soon the day came. It was a warm, sunny morning. Karina and Father left home early, as they had to meet the builder's lorry on the main road. There it was, waiting for them.

Karina felt rather shy as she climbed up among the laughing, chatting men. One of them, called Hans, made room for her on a long seat down the side. Another man, called Mr Paul, put a dear little Christmas tree into her arms.

"The roof-tree," he said. "You can look after it for us."

"Hold it tight," added Father, and Karina smiled and held it with both hands. The lorry stopped again further along, to pick up another man, but his bus was late and he kept everyone waiting.

"We'll have to hurry now, to make up for lost time," muttered Otto, the driver. He was always cross if anyone were late. With a roar of the engine, he drove off through the busy town.

He drove in and out among cars and trams and bicycles. The air was full of noise and bustle, and the smell of petrol. Everywhere, people were hurrying, hurrying on their way to work.

The lorry rattled and shook and swayed, so that Karina found it hard to stay on the seat. She had to cling to the edge with one hand to steady herself. No one was taking any notice of her now, not even Father. They were all chatting among themselves.

"You've upset Otto this morning," said someone to the man who had been late.

"Couldn't help it," he replied with a grin.

Just then, a car came out suddenly from the side entrance of a shop. Otto was not expecting this, and he had to swerve sharply. For a moment, Karina lost her balance. Then her cheeks went pink with horror. The roof-tree had gone! She just caught sight of it being crushed beneath the wheels of a furniture van! Then in a moment it was left behind and out of sight.

"The tree!" she cried. "I've dropped the tree!"

"Not surprising," muttered Mr Paul, "the way Otto is driving this morning."

"It's no good going back for it," said Father. He had seen it under the wheels of the furniture van. "Otto wouldn't stop, anyway."

"Never mind," said Hans kindly to Karina. "It wasn't your fault."

But Karina did mind. The sunny day was spoiled. The happiness had blown away on the breeze. She clung to Father's arm, and wished she had not come. The men were all silent now. Karina felt they were all cross with her for losing the tree, especially Mr Paul, who had dug it up from his own small garden.

Now there would be no roof-tree to put on the top beams of wood. There would be no blessings and good luck for the people who would live in the house. There would be no drinks for the men. Karina wished she had stayed at home with Mother.

Soon the lorry left the town behind, and came to the place where the house was being built. Everything was beautiful, just as Father had said. There were fields and wild flowers and forests all round; and in the distance there were great mountains capped with snow.

Karina could not help cheering up a little. Never had she seen anything so beautiful!

"Father," she said eagerly, "may I go for a little walk?"

"Yes," said Father, "but don't go too far. And do be careful to notice where you go, so that you can easily find your way back again."

"Yes, I'll be very careful."

Karina put her book and drawing things in a safe place. Then she started walking up the road towards the forest. She had one thing in her mind. She would find another little Christmas tree. She would dig it up, and bring it back to the men!

The air was full of the sweet smell of grass and wild flowers. Karina breathed deeply and went along a footpath until she came to the forest. She walked in a little way. There were spruce trees and fir trees and pine trees. Karina did not know one tree from another. They all looked like Christmas trees to her.

It was dark in the forest, and the sun could hardly find a space to shine through. It was quiet, and so unlike the noisy town that Karina felt lonely and a little afraid.

"I'll find a tiny tree quickly and then go back," she thought.

There was a tree, just about the size of the one she had lost. She knelt down on the soft earth and began to scrape it away. She found a sharp stone to use for digging. She had hardly started, when she thought,

"I wonder if people are allowed to dig up trees in the forest. Perhaps they are not. If they *are* allowed, why did

Mr Paul take the trouble to bring a tree all the way from his own garden?"

Now she had thought of this, Karina did not know what to do. She wanted the little tree so badly, but she had an awful feeling that digging one up was the same as stealing. The forest seemed so dark and still. She shivered. She felt unhappy and afraid.

Suddenly at that very moment, there was a great crash! There was a creak and a shudder, and all the trees began to tremble. Karina jumped to her feet in terror. She ran. Swift as the wind she ran, but in her fear, she ran deeper into the wood. She ran nearer to the noise instead of away from it.

Then all at once she saw what had happened. Some woodcutters were working. There was a pile of long, smooth, tree trunks lying near by. There was a tall, straight tree which had just been cut down. Its dark green needles were still trembling and shivering and whispering.

Two of the men began sawing off the smaller branches. Some of them looked like little trees. They were not big enough to be used for timber, and the men threw them on a pile near by. Karina stood still and watched. She smelled the sweet smell of the newly-cut trees, and listened to the singing sound of the saws.

Then one of the men caught sight of her.

"Hello," he shouted. "Would you like

a Christmas tree?" He said it for a joke because Christmas was far away. He thought the little girl would laugh and say,

"No thank you."

He was very surprised when Karina stepped forward and said,

"Oh, yes please."

So he gave her a branch that looked like a little tree.

"It's nearly as big as you are," he said. Karina said "Thank you," and she walked back the way she had come. She looked as pleased as if she were carrying the greatest treasure in the world.

. . . . . .

Meanwhile Father was on the roof of the new house. He and Hans were fixing on the topmost roof beams. Father had seen Karina walk into the forest, and he began to feel worried. He wished he had told her not to go in the forest. She might get lost.

Just then, Mr Stefan, the foreman, arrived on his motor cycle. Father heard him down below, asking Mr Paul if he had brought the roof-tree. He heard Mr Paul grumbling about the way Otto drove the lorry. He heard him telling how Karina had lost the tree.

Father gazed across at the forest again. He wished Karina would come out. Then Mr Stefan came up on the roof. He helped Father and Hans to fix the top beams. Then Hans said, with a grin,

"Doesn't look as if your little girl wasted much time."

Father looked towards the forest again. There was Karina walking along the footpath beside the fields. She was carrying a spruce tree or a fir. It was a small one, but it was nearly as big as Karina herself. She had her arms round it, holding it tightly – a tree for the roof!

So later that morning, Karina and Hans tied trails of coloured paper to its branches. Then Father and Mr Paul fixed the tree to the roof top. Then at lunch time the owner of the house came. He brought drinks for the men, and they all felt happy and excited as if it were a party.

So there, on the top of the roof, Karina's Christmas tree stood proudly, with its trails of coloured paper shivering in the breeze. There it was - the roof-tree, bringing good luck and blessings to the people who would live in the house!

Poor Old Car

Its lamps are cracked and filled with dust,
Its bumpers bent and brown with rust.
Its tyres have sunk into the ground.
Its wheels will never more go round.
Poor old car!

Its doors are swinging open wide.
Its windscreen's smashed from side to side.
It stands down there in sun and rain.
It never will drive out again.
Poor old car!

What Happened to the Forest?

This is a story from France.

Once upon a time, a man was walking home through the forest of Bessans. It was a great forest in those days, spreading far and wide. The man's wife had asked him to bring some bread back from town, so he was carrying two large loaves. They were shaped like rings, and he carried them on his arm.

He was looking forward to his supper that evening for he knew his wife would have some hot broth ready for him. It would taste good with the crisp, new bread.

Suddenly, as he walked along, something stepped silently out on the footpath in front of him. It was a wolf! It was big and thin and grey. It stared at him and growled, drawing its lips back and showing long, sharp, white teeth.

The man stood still and his heart beat fast. He was filled with fear. What could he do?

Then he thought of the bread. He slipped one of the ring-loaves from his arm and broke off a piece.

"Good evening, wolf," he said in a trembling voice. "Here is some bread for you." He threw the piece of bread as far behind him on the path as he could throw. He saw the wolf run back to find the bread.

"I've got rid of *him*," he thought, and he hurried on his way.

A few minutes later, he heard a sound behind him. It was just a small sound, a soft padding footstep and the cracking of a twig. There was the wolf again, big and thin and grey. It stared at him and growled, drawing its lips back and showing its long, sharp, white teeth.

Quickly the man broke another piece of bread from the loaf. He threw it as far behind him on the path as he could throw. The wolf ran back at once to get it, and the man hurried on his way.

He knew it would not be long before the wolf caught up with him again, so he broke off another piece of bread. Then as soon as he heard the wolf behind him, he threw the bread as before.

So the man went on through the forest, breaking bits of bread from the loaf and throwing them as far back as he could throw. The wolf also went on through the forest, following the man and running back again and again for the pieces of bread.

Very soon, one loaf was finished, and the man started breaking pieces off the other one. He was running now. He was hot and tired and panting for breath, but still the wolf followed him.

At last the man came to the end of the forest path. At last he reached his own cottage. He had only one piece of bread left, so he threw it to the wolf, saying,

"There you are, wolf. You may as well finish it." Then he went quickly into his cottage, and locked and bolted the door.

"Whatever is wrong?" asked his wife. "Why have you been running?"

"A wolf was following me," gasped the man.

"And where are the two loaves you were going to buy?" asked his wife.

"I had to give them to the wolf," he replied.

"Oh dear, what a waste of good bread," said the wife. She looked through the window, and saw the wolf sitting outside the cottage door, waiting hopefully for something else to eat.

"Wicked animal!" said the woman. She spoke in a very loud voice, and the wolf could hear everything she said. He heard her grumbling away about having to eat the broth without any bread. Then he heard her say,

"Bad animal to chase my poor husband

through the forest!" The wolf knew *she* was not likely to give him any food, so at last he crept quietly away, back into the forest of Bessans.

. . . . . .

Many months went by. During that time the man and his wife worked very hard and managed to save enough money to buy a cow. It was not enough to pay for a very good cow, but they hoped they might find an old one that would be fairly cheap.

"I'll go to market tomorrow and see what I can find," said the man. So the next morning, he walked through the forest to the town where the market was held. There were many cows for sale, and he walked up and down, looking from one to the next. They all seemed to cost rather too much money for him.

"Do you want to buy a cow?" asked someone at his side.

"Yes, I do," replied the man, "but I am looking for a cheap one. I have not much money to spend."

He looked up at the person who had spoken to him. It was a stranger. He was tall and thin, and dressed neatly in grey. His face was very unusual. It was long and pointed, and his eyes were rather close together. As he spoke, he drew his lips back and showed long, sharp, white teeth.

"I live near here," he said, "and I have lots of cows on my farm. Come with me and look at them. Perhaps you will see one that you will like."

"There's no harm in going to look," thought the man, so he went with the stranger to a big house not far from the market.

The stranger showed him a fine herd of cows.

"I will give you one for a present," he said. "You may choose the very best."

The man was so surprised that he could hardly speak, but he looked at all the cows, and he chose the one he thought was the best.

"You have chosen a very good one," said the stranger, and he tied a rope round the cow's neck, and gave her to him.

"This cow will give you good, rich milk for years to come," he said.

"Thank you," said the man, and he turned to go, but the stranger said,

"Just a moment. I have a present for your wife too." He took a little box from his pocket and gave it to the man.

"Tell your wife to open it when she is all by herself," he added.

The man was more surprised and puzzled than ever.

"Why are you so kind to me, when you do not even know me?" he asked.

"Ah, but I do know you," replied the stranger, with a smile that showed his long, sharp, white teeth. "I was once a wolf in the forest, and you fed me with all the bread you had. When people are kind to me, I am kind to them. When people are unkind to me, I am unkind to them."

The man could hardly believe his ears, but he said goodbye and went back through the forest with the cow and the little box.

"I wonder what is in the box," he thought. He walked on through the trees leading the cow, and wondering, wondering,

wondering what was in the little box.

He shook it, but he could not hear anything. He smelled it, but he could not smell anything.

"I wonder what is in it," he thought.

After a while he sat down to rest under a larch tree, with the cow standing beside him.

"I'll just peep inside the box," he thought.

Carefully he opened it, just a little way. Out sprang a great flame, leaping up to the larch tree and setting its branches on fire!

The man jumped to his feet and

pulled the cow out of danger. He wanted to put the fire out, but in a moment the whole tree was ablaze and he did not know how to start putting it out. So he thought the wisest thing to do was to hurry away.

As he walked quickly down the path, he thought,

"What a good thing *I* opened the box. If my wife had opened it, her hair and her clothes might have caught fire, and she might have been badly burned."

He hurried home and told his wife of his adventures. She was very pleased with the cow, and it gave them good, rich milk for many years.

As for the fire, it spread from one tree to the next until nearly the whole forest was burned down. And the people who live in that district say that is why there is no longer a great forest at Bessans.

Adapted

Cartwheels

There is a city in Germany where visitors are given an unusual greeting. Little boys turn cartwheels for them. They do it in the streets and squares, whenever there are a lot of people about.

The boys' fathers did just the same when they were boys. Their grandfathers did it before that, and probably their great-grandfathers and their great-great-grandfathers did it too.

No one knows for certain how the custom started, but there is a legend about it.

It is said that it started on the wedding day of a prince long ago. He was a very good ruler, and all the people loved him. They called him by a nickname, Jan Wellem.

On the day of his wedding, the city was decorated from end to end. Cannons gave a salute, and all the church bells rang. People lined the streets and cheered and waved as the wedding coach drove to the church, and then slowly back from the church to the castle.

Suddenly one of the wheels of the coach became loose. Everyone gazed in horror. For a moment it seemed that the wheel would roll away and the coach would fall.

Just then a boy ran into the road. He was ten years old. Quickly he put one hand on the hub of the wheel. Then he did cartwheels beside the coach, holding the wheel in place until it reached the end of its journey.

Then Jan Wellem stepped down from his coach and praised the boy and gave him a golden coin.

No one knows whether the story is true or not, but turning cartwheels is part of the time-table today in some of the city schools.

Every September there is a cartwheel competition for the boys of the city.
The winner is given a savings book by the mayor.

So the boys who turn cartwheels in the city today may have a few coins thrown to them by the people who watch them. Or they may win a prize when the summer ends.

The Duck Village

There was once a boy called Paul.
He lived with his mother and father at
the back of a baker's shop in a large
town. His father worked in the bakery
making the loaves and rolls. His mother
served in the shop.

Paul had no brothers and sisters, so when
the schools were on holiday he had rather
a lot of time to himself. Sometimes he
talked to his mother in the shop, but
there were usually a lot of people coming
in and out; and sooner or later his
mother would say,

"Go out in the sunshine, Paul. Walk
over the bridge and look at the ducks."
So, nearly every day in the summer, that
was what Paul did.

He walked across the bridge over the wide,
grey river. He kept to the pavement
while all the cars and buses sped along
on the road, and soon he came to the

other side where the ducks lived. He called it the Duck Village.

The ducks were not ordinary ones that came and went as they wished. They were rather special ducks, living in little wooden houses with little wooden paths leading into the water. That part of the river was cut off from the main part by a low wall.

In the Duck Village there were several different kinds of water birds. There were ducks with shining green heads and ducks with blue wings. There were ducks with wide flat bills and ducks with long pointed tails.

There were also two tall geese from China and two jet black swans from Australia. Paul liked them all, but the two he liked the best were two rather small ducks. They were called White-faced Whistling Ducks.

He liked their funny name, and he liked their funny ways. They had brown bodies, black heads and white faces, and they quacked in a strange whistling way.

Every morning a man in high rubber boots went down to the duck houses and cleaned them out with a stiff broom. Every morning he put fresh food in the feeding boxes, and waded into the water with a net to catch any bits of paper or rubbish that might have floated that way.

So Paul watched the ducks and the geese and the swans; and the summer days began to pass quickly by.

One afternoon he was standing in the baker's shop talking to his mother, when she said,

"Paul, just look after the shop while I go along to the grocer, please. I shall only be a moment."

"All right," said Paul. It was fairly quiet in the shop at that time of day, and Paul liked being left in charge sometimes. He hoped very much that someone would come in and ask for a loaf of bread, or some crisp rolls.

Someone *did* come in. Paul did not exactly see anyone walk through the open door. He did not exactly hear footsteps, but he *knew* that someone had come into the shop. He stood on his toes and peeped over the top of the counter to see who it was.

It was – he could hardly believe his eyes – it was a White-faced Whistling Duck. It flopped across the floor on its big, damp feet as if it had come in to ask for a loaf of bread or some crisp rolls.

"Well!" cried Paul, "what do *you* want?"

"Quack, quack," replied the duck in its strange, little whistling voice. Paul began to feel worried. The duck must have escaped from the Duck Village. It must have walked over the bridge near all the cars and buses and bicycles. It might easily have been run over.

Paul thought that he had better take it safely back. He grabbed hold of the duck and put it in the small room behind the shop. Just then his mother came in with her basket of shopping.

"Hello," she said. "Were there any customers?"

"Yes," said Paul. "One. It was a White-faced Whistling Duck from the Duck Village."

"Oh!" said Mother, thinking Paul was just teasing her. "Did it want a loaf of bread, or some crisp rolls?" Paul laughed.

"I'm not teasing," he said. Then he opened the door of the small room at the back of the shop, and told his mother to look.

"Well!" she exclaimed. "It *is* a duck."

The White-faced Whistling Duck flopped across the room on its big, damp feet, and did not seem worried at all.

"I shall have to take it back," said Paul.

"Will you be able to carry it?" asked

Mother. Paul picked it up and held it tightly in his arms.

"Will you be able to manage?" asked Mother. "I don't really like you to take it all by yourself, but I can't leave the shop. Come straight back, won't you?"

"Yes. I'll be all right," said Paul. He hurried out of the door and along the street towards the bridge. He *would* be all right if the duck did not wriggle.

He was lucky. The duck was very good and

very quiet. Perhaps it was a little afraid. It was rather heavy, but it kept quite still. Paul hurried across the bridge over the wide, grey river. He hurried across the bridge until he came to the Duck Village.

He looked down and saw one of the White-faced Whistling Ducks floating lazily on the water, near its own little wooden house.

"Here's your friend," said Paul, and he was just going to drop *his* White-faced Whistling Duck down beside it, when he saw something move inside the little wooden house. He waited. He stared. Then, at that moment, out of the little wooden house walked *another* White-faced Whistling Duck.

There were two White-faced Whistling Ducks as usual, so the one that Paul held in his arms did not belong to the Duck Village after all! Where *could* it have come from?

Meanwhile Paul's mother felt rather worried. The duck must be heavy for him to carry. She hoped it would not try to fly away. She hoped Paul would not run into the busy street after it.

Then she heard footsteps. Ah! Here was Paul, safely back. Here was Paul, but what was he carrying? He still held the same White-faced Whistling Duck!

"Why have you brought it back?" cried Mother.

"It didn't belong to the Duck Village," explained Paul. "There were two there as usual."

"Then where *can* it belong?"

Paul put the duck quickly into the small room at the back of the shop. Then he flopped into a chair. He was tired out.

"We'll have to look after it till we find the owner," he said.

"But how *can* we look after a duck in a house like this at the back of a baker's shop? It needs water and fresh air."

"We could let it swim in the bath," said Paul.

"Paul!" said Mother. "We can *not* keep a White-faced Whistling Duck in the bath."

Just then a man came into the shop. Mother went forward to serve him, but he did not want bread or crisp rolls.

"I'm looking for a duck," he said. "Someone told me that a little boy from this shop was carrying one. It was a very special duck –"

"A White-faced Whistling Duck?" asked Mother.

"Yes, that's right."

"Paul," called Mother. "Someone has come for the duck."

Paul came out of the small room at the back of the shop.

"Oh, you are the man who feeds the ducks in the Duck Village," he said.

"Yes. One of our White-faced Whistling Ducks escaped last night."

"But I brought it back," began Paul, "and I saw there were two there –"

"Ah! One of those is a new one," explained the man. "It arrived last night. We've been waiting a long time for it, and when we were putting it in its new home, one of the others crept out."

"Oh!" said Paul. "So now there are three."

"Yes. In fact there will soon be four. We are expecting another one to arrive this afternoon. We shall be putting another house there for the new ones."

"Well, I'm very glad," said Mother, as Paul put the duck into the man's arms. "I should *not* have liked a White-faced Whistling Duck swimming in our bath even for one day."

. . . . . .

Next spring, when Paul was leaning over the bridge looking at the Duck Village, the man came along with the food bucket.

"Hello," he said. "Your White-faced Whistling Duck has a family of babies now. Would you like to see them?"

"Yes, please," said Paul. He went down with the man and peeped into the little wooden house. There he saw the White-faced Whistling Duck fussing over some little bundles of fluff.

"Quack, quack," she said in her strange little whistling voice, as if she were saying to her family,

"This is Paul. He is a friend of mine."

The Three Golden Hairs – Part 1

Once upon a time, there was a boy who was born under a lucky star. His mother and father were very poor, but they said to their friends,

"Our son has been born under a lucky star, and no harm will come to him. Who knows, he might even marry the king's daughter!"

Now a few days later it happened that the king himself rode into that village. He heard the people talking about the new baby. He heard them say,

"The baby in that cottage was born under a lucky star. When he grows up he will marry the king's daughter."

The king's daughter was also a baby at that time, and the king thought to himself,

"He will certainly not marry my daughter. I will see to that." So he went to the parents of the child. They did not know he was the king, but they could see he was a very rich man. He looked at the baby and said,

"How I should love to have a little son like that. Let me take him. I can give him everything he will ever need."

"Oh, no," replied the mother.

The king asked again and again. Then at last the father said to the mother,

"Our son would have a much happier life with this rich man. Why! We hardly ever have enough food even for ourselves." So they laid the baby in the box they used as a cradle and they gave him to the king.

The king carried the box on his horse and rode on his way. He was a wicked man and he meant to drown the child. So when he had left the village far behind, he threw the box into the river and rode away.

For a moment it seemed as if the box would overturn. Then it was caught in the current and it went sailing down the river like a little boat.

Soon afterwards a miller saw it floating towards his cottage. He held out a long pole and managed to pull the box into the shore. How surprised he was to find a baby boy inside!

He and his wife had no children of their own, and they thought the child had been sent to them from Heaven. They loved him and cared for him, and as the years passed, he grew into a fine, strong boy.

One day when the boy was thirteen, the

king came that way. He stopped to speak to the miller and, seeing the boy standing near, he said,

"Is that your son?"

"Not really," replied the miller, "though he is like a son to us. We found him as a baby, floating in a box down the river."

The king guessed at once that this was the child he had tried to drown, so he said,

"He looks a fine, strong boy. Will you let him take a letter to the queen for me?"

"Certainly, Your Majesty," replied the miller. So a little later the boy set off towards the town where the king's palace was. He was proud to be taking a letter from the king to the queen, but of course, he did not know what was written in it. It said,

"Let the boy who brings this letter be cast into prison as soon as he arrives."

The boy walked a long way, and by evening he came to a lonely forest.

Darkness was falling and he was very tired, but soon he saw a small cottage. He knocked at the door and an old woman opened it.

"Please may I stay here for the night?" asked the boy. "I am taking a letter from the king to the queen, and I will leave early in the morning."

"You may stay if you wish," said the woman, "but I must warn you that the cottage belongs to some robbers and they may be angry when they find you here."

"I'm not afraid," said the boy; and he lay down in the corner and fell asleep.

Soon the robbers returned.

"Who is this?" they asked, staring at him.

"It is just a poor boy taking a letter from the king to the queen," replied the old woman. "He will leave here early in the morning."

"Let's open the letter," said one of the robbers. "There may be money in it."

He opened the letter and read it to the
others,

"Let the boy who brings this letter be
cast into prison as soon as he arrives."

Then the robbers felt sorry for the
boy so they tore the letter to bits,
and wrote a new one. This one said,

"Let the boy who brings this letter
be married to the princess as soon as he
arrives."

The boy slept all night. Then early

next morning he left the robbers' cottage and went on his way. He quickly reached the palace and gave the letter to the queen. The queen opened it and read,

"Let the boy who brings this letter be married to the princess as soon as he arrives."

If the queen were surprised, she did not say so. Besides, both she and the princess liked the boy as soon as they saw him, so a wedding was arranged at once.

For a few weeks the boy lived very happily in the palace. Then the king returned and was, of course, very angry.

"You have married the princess," he said, "but you cannot keep her unless you bring me three golden hairs from the head of the giant who lives in the cave beyond the lake."

"All right," replied the boy. "I will do so."

He said goodbye to the queen and the princess and he walked until he came to the gates of a city.

"Who are you, and what do you know?" asked the guard.

"I am married to the princess," replied the boy, "and I know everything."

"Then tell us why our fountain no longer gives us water."

"Let me pass through, and I will tell you when I return," said the boy. He walked on and on, and soon he came to the gates of another city.

"Who are you, and what do you know?" asked the guard.

"I am married to the princess," replied the boy, "and I know everything."

"Then tell us why the tree that used to bear golden apples now bears no apples at all."

"Let me pass through, and I will tell you when I return," said the boy. He walked on and on and soon he came to a large lake. He saw a ferry-man waiting in a rowing boat.

"Who are you, and what do you know?"

asked the ferry-man.

"I am married to the princess," replied the boy, "and I know everything."

"Then tell me why I have to row people across this lake from morning till night," said the ferry-man. "What can I do to set myself free?"

"Row me across, and I will tell you when I return," said the boy.

The Three Golden Hairs
– Part 2

So the ferry-man rowed him to the other side and the boy walked on until he came at last to the cave where the giant lived. The giant was out, but his grandmother sat in the entrance.

"Who are you, and what do you want?" she asked the boy.

"I am married to the princess and I want three golden hairs from the head of the giant," he answered.

"I will try to help you," said the grandmother kindly.

"There is something else I want," added the boy. "I want to know why the fountain of the first city has run dry. I want to know why the apple tree that bore golden apples in the second city now bears no apples at all. I want to know what the ferry-man at the lake can do to set himself free."

Then the grandmother turned the boy into an ant and hid him in the folds of her skirt. There he stayed and listened all night.

Soon the giant came home to the cave. He ate a meal and then fell asleep with his head in the grandmother's lap.

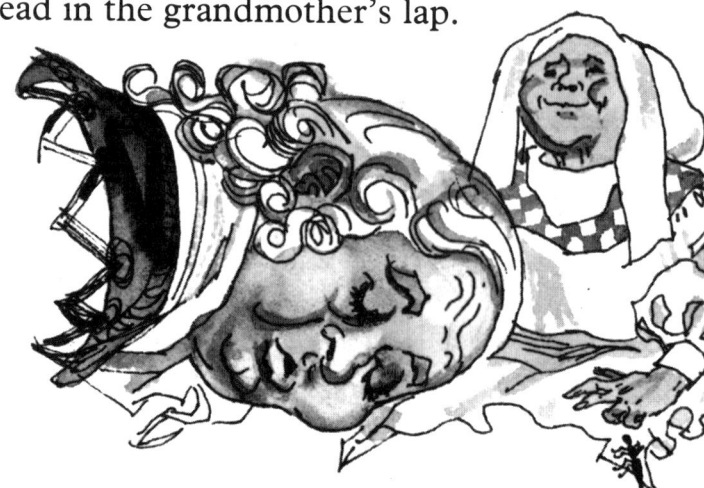

Suddenly, tweak! The grandmother pulled out one golden hair.

"What is wrong?" cried the giant, waking angrily.

"I had a strange dream," replied the grandmother, "and I awoke in a fright and caught hold of your hair."

"What did you dream?" asked the giant.

"I dreamed of a fountain that had run dry, and I wondered why."

"That is easy to answer," said the giant. "If the people of the city would take away the frog that sits at the mouth of the fountain, the water would flow as before."

When the giant had spoken, he fell asleep again with his head on the grandmother's lap.

Then, tweak! She pulled out a second golden hair.

"What is wrong?" cried the giant, waking angrily.

"I had a strange dream," replied the

grandmother, "and I awoke in a fright and caught hold of your hair."

"What did you dream?" asked the giant.

"I dreamed of an apple tree that once bore golden apples and now bears no apples at all, and I wondered why."

"That is easy to answer," said the giant. "If the people of the city would take away the mouse that gnaws at the root of the tree, it would bear golden apples as before."

Again the giant fell asleep with his head on the grandmother's lap. Then, tweak! She pulled out a third golden hair.

"What is wrong now?" cried the giant, waking angrily.

"I had another strange dream," replied the grandmother. "I dreamed of a ferry-man who has to row people across a lake from morning till night, and I wondered what he could do to set himself free."

"That is easy to answer," said the

giant. "If he were to put the oar into the hand of someone else, then that person would have to take his place, and he would be free. Now stop dreaming and let me sleep in peace."

So the boy had the answers to the three questions, and early in the morning the grandmother changed him back to his own shape and gave him the three golden hairs. He thanked her and set off back towards the palace.

Soon he came to the lake. He saw the ferry-man waiting with the rowing boat.

"What is the answer to my question?" asked the ferry-man.

"I will tell you when you have rowed me across," replied the boy. Then, as soon as the boat reached the other side, he jumped ashore and said,

"If you put the oar into the hand of someone else, then that person will have to take your place, and you will be free."

"Thank you," cried the ferry-man.

Soon the boy came to the city where the apple tree grew.

"Take away the mouse that gnaws at the root of the tree," he said, "and the tree will bear golden apples as before." The people of the city were so pleased that they gave him a donkey laden with gold.

Soon he came to the city where the fountain had run dry.

"Take away the frog that sits at the

mouth of the fountain," he said, "and the water will flow as before." The people were so pleased that they gave him another donkey laden with gold, and so at last he came back to the palace.

The queen and the princess were very glad to see him, and the king was amazed when the boy handed him the three golden hairs from the head of the giant.

"And all this gold!" cried the king, pointing to the laden donkeys. "Where did you get it?"

"On the far side of a lake," replied the boy. "I brought only a little of it because there was far too much to carry."

"Tell me where it is," said the king, "so that I can go and get some as well." The boy told him where to find the lake.

"Ask the ferry-man to row you across," he added, "and you will find the gold on the other side."

So the king went to the lakeside and asked the ferry-man to row him across.

"Certainly," said the ferry-man and as soon as they had reached the other side he put the oar into the king's hands and jumped ashore. So the ferry-man became free at last, and the wicked king became the ferry-man. He had to row people across the lake from morning till night, from morning till night; and for all I know, he is doing it still.

As for the boy who was born under a lucky star, he and the princess of course, lived happily ever after.

Adapted